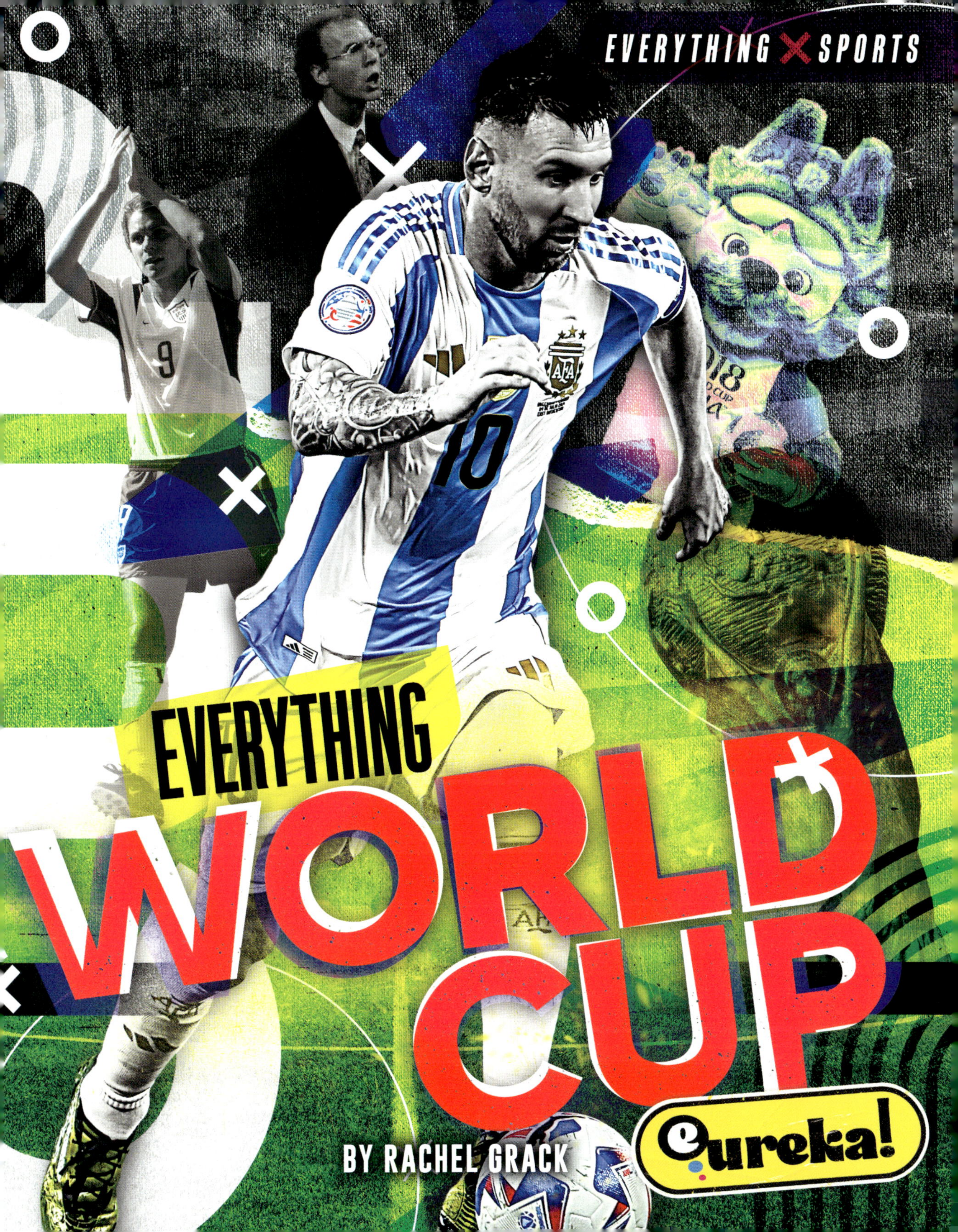
EVERYTHING SPORTS
EVERYTHING
WORLD CUP
BY RACHEL GRACK
eureka!

Eureka! books turn real stories into unforgettable experiences. This nonfiction imprint sparks curiosity, encourages critical thinking, and engages middle-grade readers. *Eureka!* books empower young minds to explore the stories of the real world, one fascinating fact at a time. Unravel the power of knowledge and lifelong learning with *Eureka!*

This edition first published in 2026 by Bellwether Media, Inc.

Library of Congress Cataloging-in-Publication Data

Names: Koestler-Grack, Rachel A., 1973- author
Title: Everything World Cup / Rachel Grack.
Description: Eureka!. | Minneapolis, Minnesota : Bellwether Media, Inc, 2026. | Series: Everything sports | Includes index. | Audience: Ages 9-15 | Audience: Grades 7-9 | Summary: "Engaging images accompany information on the World Cup. The text level and subject matter are intended for students in grades 5 through 9" -- Provided by publisher.
Identifiers: LCCN 2025028074 (print) | LCCN 2025028075 (ebook) | ISBN 9798893045635 library binding | ISBN 9798893047011 ebook
Subjects: LCSH: World Cup (Soccer)--Juvenile literature | Soccer teams--Juvenile literature | Soccer--History--Juvenile literature
Classification: LCC GV943.49 .K64 2026 (print) | LCC GV943.49 (ebook) | DDC 796.334/66809--dc23/eng/20250613
LC record available at https://lccn.loc.gov/2025028074
LC ebook record available at https://lccn.loc.gov/2025028075

Editor: Kieran Downs Designer: Jeffrey Kollock

Printed in the United States of America, North Mankato, MN.

TABLE OF CONTENTS

PENALTY SHOOTOUT	4
WHAT IS THE WORLD CUP?	6
WORLD CUP HISTORY	12
TERRIFIC TEAMS	18
WORLD CUP GREATS	26
MEMORABLE MOMENTS	38
THE WORLD CUP BY THE NUMBERS	44
GLOSSARY	46
WRITE ABOUT IT!	47
INDEX	48

PENALTY SHOOTOUT

At the end of **regulation time**, the score of the 2022 World Cup final is tied 2–2. Soccer legend Lionel Messi is hoping to lift his first World Cup trophy. He soon scores a goal for Argentina. About 10 minutes later, France's Kylian Mbappé scores, giving him a **hat trick** for the match. The game is tied again. As extra time runs out, the game remains deadlocked. A **penalty shootout** will decide the winner.

The players line up on the **pitch**. Each team takes turns at a best-of-five chance on goals. Mbappé gets the first kick for France. He fires it past Argentina goalkeeper Emi Martínez. Messi is up next for Argentina. His kick rolls right in. France takes a second kick. This one is **saved** by Martínez! Argentina scores their second kick to take a 2–1 lead on penalties. The third kick by France goes wide. Argentina narrowly makes its third kick. France nets their fourth shot to stay in the game. Argentina's Gonzalo Montiel goes next. The ball sails into the left side of the net. Goal! Argentina wins 4–2 on penalty kicks. In his fifth appearance in a World Cup final, Messi nets a victory!

HISTORIC HAT TRICK

Kylian Mbappé is only the second player to ever score a hat trick in the World Cup final. The first player was England's Geoff Hurst in 1966.

MESSI'S
PENALTY SHOT

WHAT IS THE WORLD CUP?

The World Cup is an international soccer **tournament**. It is organized by the Fédération Internationale de Football Association (FIFA). The association currently includes 211 national soccer teams. Teams compete for a **ticket** to participate in the World Cup tournament. This monthlong event takes place every four years. Brazil holds the most men's World Cup championships with five. It is also the only men's team to have played in every tournament. In 2019, the United States women's team won their fourth championship, giving them the most Women's World Cup wins.

FIFA WORLD CUP CONTINENTAL ZONES

UEFA

CONCACAF

CONMEBOL

CAF

AFC

OFC

FIFA is divided into six **confederations**. AFC includes all of Asia and Australia. CAF covers all of Africa. CONCACAF consists of North America, Central America, and the Caribbean. CONMEBOL is made up of teams from South America. OFC contains teams from Oceania. UEFA includes teams from Europe. For each World Cup, FIFA decides the number of finals tickets given to each of the confederations. The number of tickets is based on the strength of the teams, as well as **lobbying** from the confederations. The nation or nations hosting the World Cup automatically qualify for the tournament. As of the 2026 World Cup, all six confederations were guaranteed at least one **berth**.

The World Cup starts with qualifier matches. These games can start as early as three years before the World Cup and play out over a two-year period. The format differs slightly for men and women. Each confederation has its own schedule for sets of matches and qualifying rounds. Some regions play head-to-head matches while other regions do tournaments. Teams play one another for points. A win is worth three points, a **draw** is one point, and a loss is zero points. The teams with the most points advance to the World Cup.

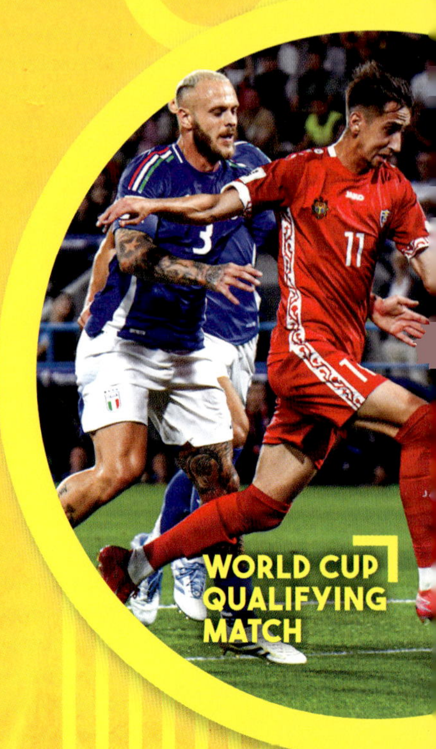
WORLD CUP QUALIFYING MATCH

Six teams get a second chance to make the World Cup through the FIFA Play-Off Tournament. The Play-Off includes one team from each confederation plus an extra team from the host confederation based on the FIFA World Rankings. The four lowest-ranked nations in the tournament play matches in **bracket** semifinals. The two highest-ranked teams go directly into the Play-Off finals. The winners of the semifinals play against the teams with higher **seeds** in the finals. These winners advance to the World Cup. The women's tournament features 32 teams, with plans to expand to 48 teams by 2031. The men's tournament expanded to include 48 teams in the 2026 World Cup.

WORLD CUP AWARDS

GOLDEN BALL

An award given to the best player in a World Cup

PLAY-OFF MATCH

GOLDEN BOOT

An award given to the top goal scorer in a World Cup

GOLDEN GLOVE

An award given to the best goalkeeper in a World Cup

GROUP STAGE MATCH

At the World Cup, teams first compete in the **group stage**. They are split into groups of four teams. As of 2026, the group stage consists of 12 groups of four teams. Each group gets randomly selected out of **pots**. Teams are divided into different pots based on their rankings. Each group gets one team from each pot. Teams play one match against each of the other teams in their group. They earn points the same way as in the qualifying rounds, with a win gaining three points and a draw gaining one. The two teams with the most points from each group advance to the **knockout stage**. The top eight third-place teams also advance to the next round.

GROUP DRAW

In the knockout stage, teams play elimination matches until only one team is left in the group. Finally, only two teams remain for the final match, one of which will become the World Cup champion. A third-place match takes place between the losers of the semifinal games.

KNOCKOUT STAGE MATCH

2022 WORLD CUP KNOCKOUT STAGE BRACKET

WORLD CUP HISTORY

FIFA was founded in 1904 with seven national associations. These associations were from Belgium, Denmark, France, Spain, Sweden, Switzerland, and the Netherlands. French journalist Robert Guérin became its first president. Before the World Cup, the biggest international soccer tournament took place at the Summer Olympics. In 1921, Jules Rimet became FIFA's third president. Rimet decided soccer should have its own championship tournament. He proposed the idea of a World Cup every four years starting in 1930.

Uruguay offered to host the first **quadrennial** tournament. Thirteen nations participated. There were seven from South America, four from Europe, and two from North America. In the final match, Uruguay defeated Argentina 4–2, becoming the first nation to win a World Cup. The 1930 World Cup featured group phases. In 1934 and 1938, teams advanced straight to the knockout stage. The 1942 and 1946 tournaments were canceled due to World War II. The World Cup resumed in 1950, but fewer teams attended. It was the only World Cup to replace knockout stages with two group phases.

1930 WORLD CUP POSTER

FIRST GOAL

Lucien Laurent of France scored the first goal in World Cup history.

1930 WORLD CUP

1950 WORLD CUP STADIUM, BRAZIL

The 1954 World Cup was the first soccer tournament to be televised. This tournament featured 16 teams. They were split into four groups of four teams. The top two teams in each group advanced to the quarterfinals. However, teams did not play the other teams in their group. Instead, two seeded groups played the other two groups.

In 1958, FIFA changed the format slightly again. Each nation played the other three teams in its group. The top teams qualified for the next round.

1954 WORLD CUP

1970 WORLD CUP

In 1970, Brazil became the first country to win three World Cups. For their achievement, the team was permanently awarded the Jules Rimet Trophy. A new World Cup trophy was created for the 1974 tournament in West Germany.

The 1974 and 1978 tournaments had some new format changes. The quarterfinals and semifinals were replaced by a second group phase. This round was made up of two groups of four teams. The top nation in each group advanced to the final. Runners-up played each other for third place.

In 1982, the tournament expanded to 24 teams. In 1986, the second group stage was replaced with the current knockout stage. The World Cup expanded again in 1998 to 32 teams. The World Cup expanded to 48 teams for the 2026 event, with 32 reaching the knockout stage.

1998 WORLD CUP

RECORD-SETTING WORLD CUP

The 1954 World Cup set all-time goal-scoring records. The 26-game tournament averaged a record 5.38 goals per game.

The first unofficial world soccer championship for women took place in Italy in 1970. It was sponsored by the Martini & Rossi beverage company. Many other smaller tournaments took place throughout the 1980s. In 1988, FIFA organized an invitational tournament. It took place in China with 12 teams. The tournament was so successful that FIFA decided to hold an official world championship for women in 1991. The U.S. beat Norway 2–1 in the final, becoming the first official Women's World Cup champions. The success of the Women's World Cup led to a quadrennial tournament.

Since then, the Women's World Cup has grown in size and popularity. In 1995, the tournament increased playtime from 80 minutes to 90 minutes. In 1999, the tournament included 16 teams. Prize money was added to the 2007 Women's World Cup with the winning team awarded $1 million. That amount increased in later tournaments. In 2015, FIFA expanded the tournament to 24 teams. In 2023, the tournament expanded to 32 teams. The winning team was awarded $4.29 million.

TIMELINE

1904
FIFA is founded

1930
The first World Cup is played in Uruguay

1942
The World Cup is canceled due to World War II

1982
The World Cup expands to 24 teams

1988
FIFA holds a women's invitational tournament in China

1991
The first official Women's World Cup tournament takes place

1998
The World Cup expands to a 32-team competition

1999
The Women's World Cup expands to 16 teams

2023
The Women's World Cup expands to 32 teams

2026
The World Cup features 48 teams

VICTORY STARS

Teams who have won the World Cup have stars added to their team's logo on their jerseys. Each star represents one victory.

TERRIFIC TEAMS

1970 BRAZIL

The Brazil national team of 1970 showcased some of the greatest talent in World Cup history. Brazil's front five players of Jairzinho, Pelé, Gérson, Tostão, and Rivellino created an unstoppable attacking force. The team won all six of its qualifying matches, scoring 23 goals while giving up only two.

In the World Cup, Brazil went undefeated in group play, including a win over reigning World Cup champion England. They defeated Peru in the quarterfinals 4–2. In the semifinals, Brazil defeated Uruguay 3–1. Brazil met Italy in the final. Brazil took the match in a 4–1 victory thanks to goals from Pelé, Gérson, Jairzinho, and Carlos Alberto.

This was Brazil's third title, following victories in 1958 and 1962. As the first team to win three World Cups, Brazil became the world's most successful national soccer team. At the first World Cup in 1930, FIFA agreed that if any nation won three World Cups, they would be given the trophy to keep. Brazil became permanent holders of the Jules Rimet Trophy for their accomplishment.

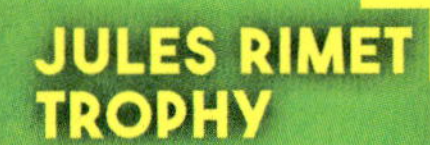

JULES RIMET TROPHY

MISSING TROPHY

The Jules Rimet Trophy was stolen in 1983 while on display in Rio de Janeiro. It remains missing.

SUPER STAR
JAIRZINHO
POSITION
FORWARD
PELÉ
KEY STAT
7 GOALS
WORLD CUP RECORD
WIN DRAW LOSS
6—0—0
GOALS FOR
19
GOALS AGAINST
7
ORDEM E P

1974 WEST GERMANY

The 1974 West Germany national team was known for its **tactical** skills and strong defense. The team was led by midfielder Franz Beckenbauer. Other talented players included goalkeeper Sepp Maier, backs Berti Vogts and Paul Breitner, and goal-pounding forward Gerd Müller. They entered the World Cup as reigning European champions.

The 1974 World Cup featured two group stages. In the first group stage, West Germany won their first two games before losing to East Germany. The team still qualified for the second group round, where they went undefeated. This qualified the team for the final.

The final was held in Munich, West Germany. West Germany faced off against the Netherlands team led by fierce attacker Johan Cruyff. The Netherlands took an early lead. In the 25th minute, Breitner scored on a penalty to tie the game 1–1. Müller netted another goal for West Germany in the 43rd minute to give West Germany the lead. The Netherlands fought back with dazzling attacks. But time after time, the West Germany defense kept them from scoring. The clock ticked down to zero. West Germany secured a 2–1 victory. They became the first team to win both the European Championship and the World Cup back-to-back.

SEPP MAIER

SUPER STAR

GERD MÜLLER

POSITION

FORWARD

KEY STAT

4 GOALS

WORLD CUP RECORD

WIN DRAW LOSS

6–0–1

GOALS FOR

13

GOALS AGAINST

4

2010 SPAIN

XABI ALONSO

The 2010 Spain squad dominated opponents with their tiki-taka style of play. This extremely technical tactic uses many short, quick passes to maintain possession of the ball. Team Spain was loaded with talent. Midfielders Xabi Alonso, Andrés Iniesta, and Xavi were some of the best passers in the game. For scoring power, the team had forward David Villa. His five goals in the 2010 World Cup earned him the Silver Boot award. Goalkeeper Iker Casillas was known for making miracle saves. He gave up only two goals at the 2010 World Cup.

Spain won all of its 2010 World Cup qualifying matches. As the 2008 European champions, they entered the tournament as the favorite to win. But they suffered a shocking defeat in their first match against Switzerland. They bounced back to win their next two group stage matches. Spain defeated Paraguay in the quarterfinals and Germany in the semifinals to reach their first ever final. The match against the Netherlands went through regulation time without a goal from either side. In extra time, the Netherlands were down a player due to penalties. In the 116th minute, Iniesta found the far corner to score the winning goal. Spain took its first World Cup with a 1–0 victory.

ANDRÉS INIESTA'S WINNING GOAL

WORLD CUP RECORD

WIN 6 — DRAW 0 — LOSS 1

GOALS FOR 8

GOALS AGAINST 2

SUPER STAR

IKER CASILLAS

2015 UNITED STATES WOMEN'S NATIONAL TEAM

At the 2011 Women's World Cup, the U.S. finished second after a heartbreaking defeat to Japan. The team was ready for a rematch. The 2015 U.S. team featured talented veterans such as forwards Abby Wambach and Alex Morgan, midfielder Megan Rapinoe, and goalkeeper Hope Solo.

In the group stage, the U.S. won two matches and drew one game while allowing only one goal. In the knockout stage, the U.S. defeated Columbia 2–0, China 1–0, and Germany 2–0. The wins were part of a 540-minute scoreless streak that earned Solo the Golden Glove for the second tournament in a row.

The U.S. faced Japan in the final match. In the 3rd minute, midfielder Carli Lloyd scored off of a corner kick from Rapinoe to give the U.S. the lead. Two minutes later, Lloyd scored again. In the 16th minute, Lloyd scored her third goal to net the first ever hat trick in a women's World Cup final. Midfielder Lauren Holiday and forward Tobin Heath each added a goal. Japan only scored twice. The 5–2 U.S. victory gave the team its third Women's World Cup, the most wins by any country. With six goals in seven matches, Lloyd tied for top scorer in the tournament and earned the Golden Ball.

MEGAN RAPINOE

SUPER STAR
CARLI LLOYD
POSITION
MIDFIELDER
KEY STAT
6 GOALS
ALEX MORGAN
WORLD CUP RECORD
WIN DRAW LOSS
6—1—0
GOALS FOR
14
GOALS AGAINST
3

WORLD CUP GREATS

Known by his nickname, Pelé was one of the greatest soccer players of all time. He first played for the Brazil national team at age 16. At the 1958 World Cup in Sweden, he drew world attention. He became the youngest person ever to score in a World Cup with his first goal against Wales. He scored a hat trick in the semifinal against France and netted two more goals in Brazil's victory over Sweden in the final.

During the second match of the 1962 World Cup, Pelé suffered a torn thigh muscle. He sat out the final rounds as Brazil claimed its second World Cup title. A leg injury sidelined Pelé again for the 1966 World Cup in England. Without their star player, Brazil did not make it past the group stage. Pelé returned for the 1970 World Cup in Mexico. He scored four goals, including one in the final for a 4–1 victory over Italy. He became the second person in history to score in four World Cups. His six assists in the 1970 World Cup are a record. He remains the only athlete to have won three World Cups. Pelé's spectacular skills and style of play helped put soccer and the World Cup in the global spotlight.

PROFILE

HEIGHT 5 FT 8 IN

BIRTHDAY OCTOBER 23, 1940

POSITIONS MIDFIELDER, FORWARD

WORLD CUPS 1958, 1962, 1966, 1970

TEAM BRAZIL

FAMOUS NAME

Pelé's full birth name is Edson Arantes do Nascimento. His parents named him after the famous inventor Thomas Edison.

AWARDS & RECORDS

- 14 MATCHES
- 12 GOALS
- 10 ASSISTS
- 1,260 MINUTES
- 3 WORLD CUP CHAMPIONSHIPS
- 1 GOLDEN BALL
- 1 SILVER BALL

Diego Maradona was one of the best soccer players of the 1980s. He is known for his memorable goals. His pure love for the game earned him the nickname "The Golden Boy." At 16, he became the youngest player to take the field for the Argentine national team. Maradona played for Argentina in four World Cups between 1982 and 1994.

DIEGO MARADONA

PLAYER #10

Maradona scored two goals at the 1982 World Cup in Spain. His most dominant performance was at the 1986 tournament. He scored two memorable goals in the quarterfinals against England. The first goal bounced off his hand, which was an illegal move. But the referee mistakenly thought the ball had struck Maradona's head. For the second goal, Maradona masterfully **dribbled** through a group of defenders to score. Argentina went on to beat West Germany in the final. Maradona finished the tournament with five goals and the Golden Ball. In 1990, he helped Argentina finish second to West Germany and was awarded the Bronze Ball. He scored another goal at the 1994 World Cup in the U.S. But Argentina fell to Romania in the knockout stage. Maradona retired in 1997. During his World Cup career, he scored eight goals in 21 matches.

PROFILE

HEIGHT 5 FT 5 IN

BIRTHDAY OCTOBER 30, 1960

POSITION MIDFIELDER

WORLD CUPS

1982, 1986, 1990, 1994

TEAM  ARGENTINA

AWARDS & RECORDS

21 MATCHES

8 GOALS

8 ASSISTS

1,936 MINUTES

1 WORLD CUP CHAMPIONSHIP

1 GOLDEN BALL

1 BRONZE BALL

1 SILVER BOOT

PLAYER OF THE CENTURY

In 1999, FIFA jointly awarded Maradona and Pelé the Player of the Century award.

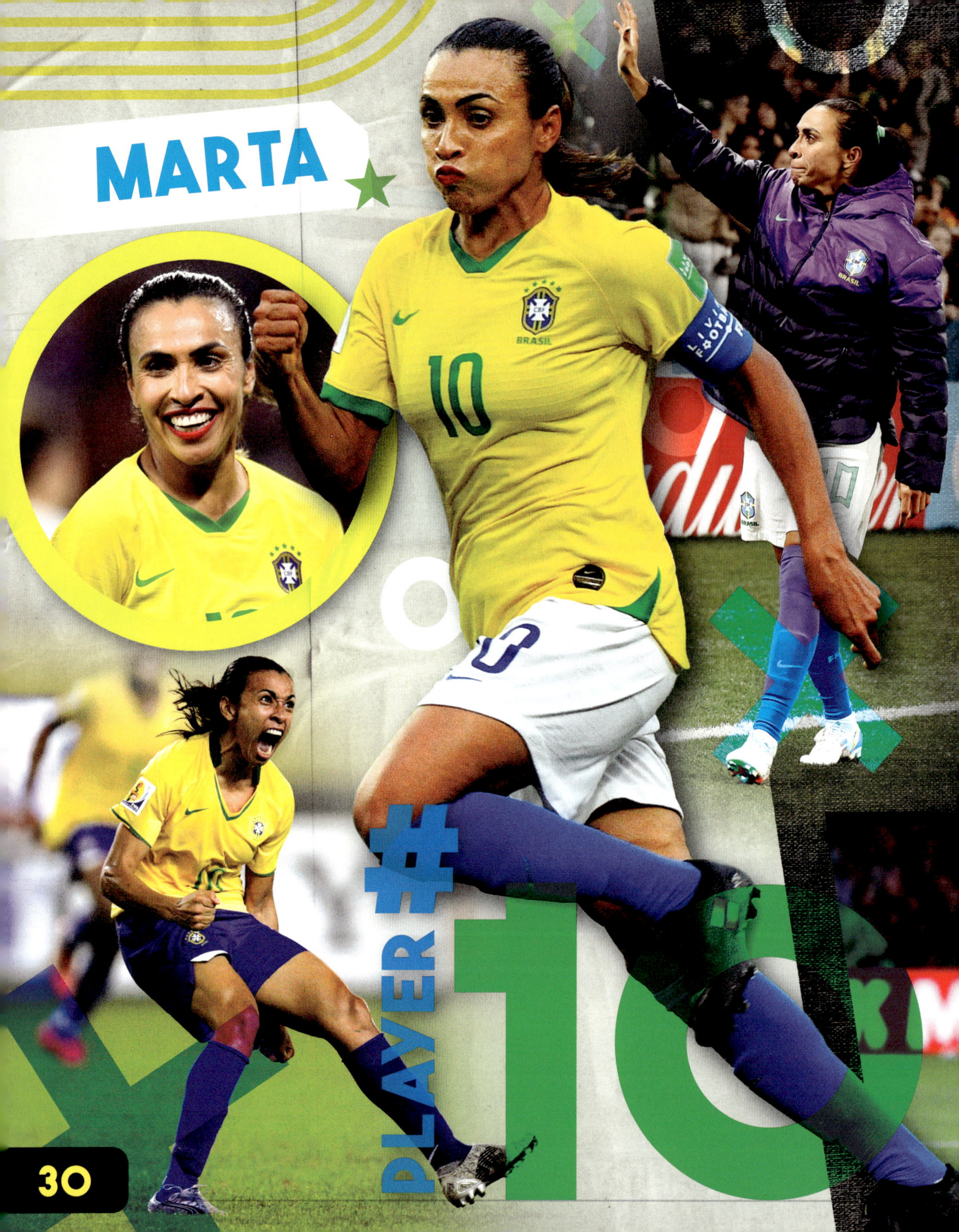
MARTA
PLAYER #10

Marta is one of the greatest women's soccer players of all time. She started playing internationally at age 16 as part of Brazil's Under-20 Women's World Cup team. She joined the senior national team for the 2003 Women's World Cup. She scored three goals in the tournament, but Brazil was knocked out in the quarterfinals. At the 2007 Women's World Cup, Marta scored seven goals and helped lead Brazil to a second-place finish. Her performance at the tournament earned her the Golden Ball for best player and the Golden Boot as the leading goal scorer. She scored four more goals and added two more assists at the 2011 Women's World Cup. But Brazil was again eliminated in the quarterfinals. In 2015, she scored her 15th World Cup goal. It made her the player with the most career goals ever scored in Women's World Cup history.

At the 2019 Women's World Cup, Marta netted her 17th World Cup goal. This score made her the top World Cup goal scorer for both men and women. But Brazil lost in the Round of 16. In 2023, Brazil was eliminated in the group stage. Even without a World Cup win, Marta remains one of the best players in the world.

BIRTHDAY FEBRUARY 19, 1986

POSITION FORWARD

WORLD CUPS AS OF 2025: 2003, 2007, 2011, 2015, 2019, 2023

TEAM BRAZIL

FIVE WORLD CUP GOALS

Marta scored goals in five World Cup tournaments. Only two other players have accomplished this feat in men's and women's World Cup tournaments.

AWARDS & RECORDS

AS OF 2025

1 GOLDEN BALL

1 GOLDEN BOOT

1 SILVER BOOT

LIONEL
MESSI
PLAYER #10

Many consider Lionel Messi the greatest soccer player of all time. He received eight Ballon d'Or awards as FIFA's best player in the world. But he faced many World Cup disappointments playing for the national team of his home country Argentina.

Messi scored his first World Cup goal in his first World Cup appearance in 2006. At the 2010 World Cup, he helped Argentina reach the quarterfinals, where they were eliminated by Germany. In 2014, Messi scored four goals to lead Argentina back to the final. But they lost to Germany again. Messi earned the Golden Ball for his outstanding performance. At the 2018 World Cup, Messi scored a goal and had two assists. But Argentina was knocked out by France. At last, in 2022, Argentina captured the World Cup trophy in a thrilling penalty shootout victory over France. Messi had three assists and scored seven goals in the tournament.

During his World Cup career, Messi has set numerous records. These include most goals by a player on the Argentina team, most Player of the Match awards, and second-most World Cup match victories. His 26 World Cup match appearances are the most by any player. He is also the only player with an assist in five different World Cups.

THE KICKS

Morgan wrote a series of soccer books for middle schoolers called *The Kicks*. Its stories spotlight the importance of teamwork. The series was adapted into a TV show in 2015.

Alex Morgan is one of the top goal scorers in U.S. women's soccer history. At the 2011 Women's World Cup, she played five matches and scored two goals. One of those goals was in the final against Japan. But the U.S. lost the match in a penalty shootout.

In 2015, Morgan played in all seven games to help the U.S. win the Women's World Cup for the first time since 1999. At the 2019 Women's World Cup, Morgan scored five goals in the opening match against Thailand for a 13–0 win. This tied the record for most individual goals in a single game. The U.S. went on to win its second straight World Cup title. Morgan finished the tournament with six goals and three assists, earning the Silver Boot. Morgan returned for the 2023 Women's World Cup. But the U.S. was eliminated in the Round of 16. Morgan retired from professional soccer in 2024. During her career, she was an important part of making the U.S. a powerhouse team.

BIRTHDAY JULY 2, 1989

POSITION FORWARD

WORLD CUPS

2011, 2015, 2019, 2023

UNITED STATES

AWARDS & RECORDS

22 MATCHES

9 GOALS

5 ASSISTS

1,478 MINUTES

2 WORLD CUP CHAMPIONSHIPS

1 SILVER BOOT

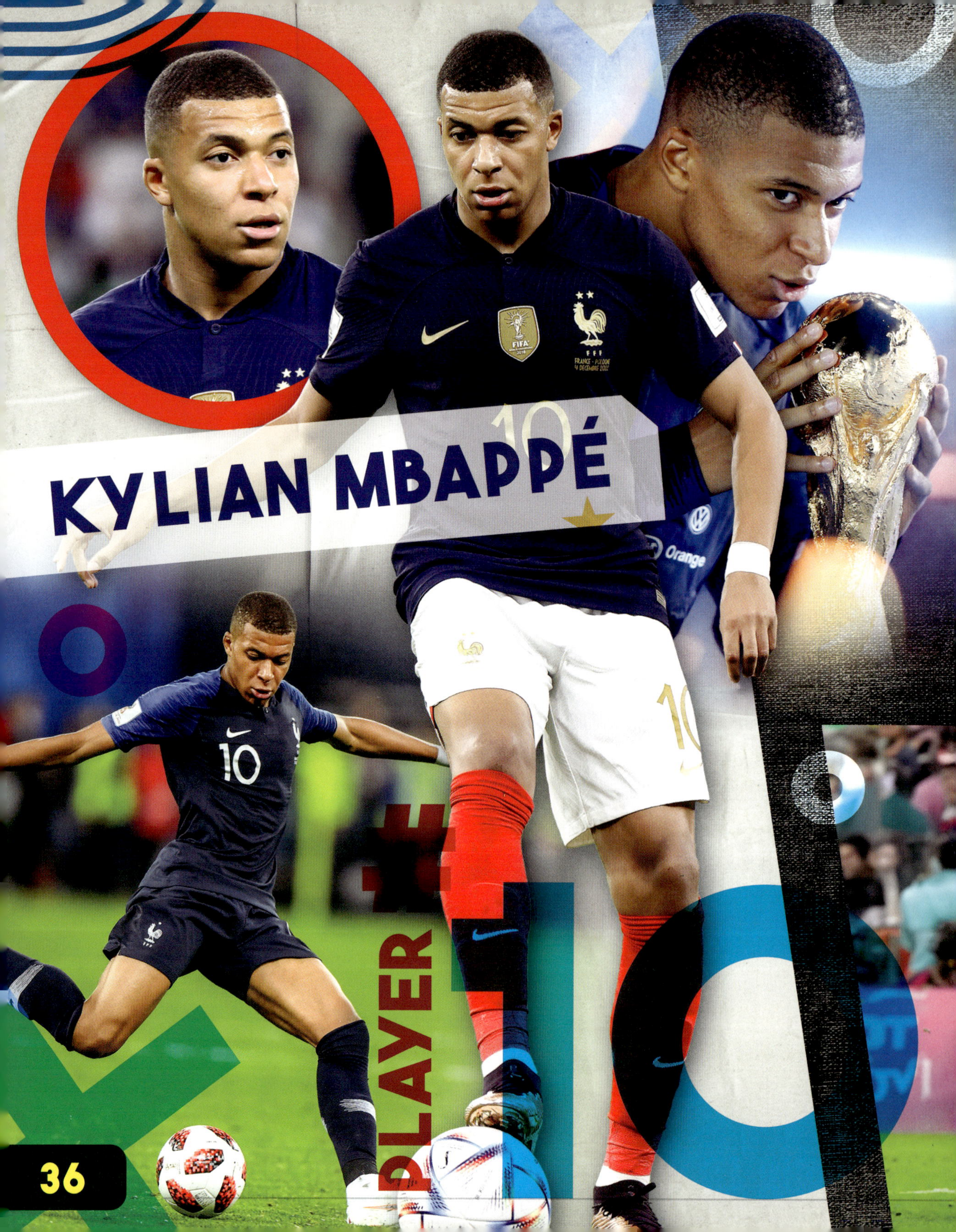
KYLIAN MBAPPÉ
PLAYER #10

Kylian Mbappé is best known for his speed and dribbling skills. At 19 years old, Mbappé played for France in the 2018 World Cup. He scored four goals in the World Cup, including the only goal in France's 1-0 group stage win over Peru. He was the youngest French player to score a goal in World Cup history. Mbappé also scored a goal in the final match against Croatia, helping France secure a 4-2 victory and win the World Cup. He won the World Cup award for Best Young Player.

At the 2022 World Cup, Mbappé scored eight goals in seven matches, more than any other player that year. He earned the tournament's Golden Boot award as well as the Silver Ball as second-best player. He helped lead France to the final match. In the final, Mbappé scored three goals, but France lost to Argentina on penalty kicks. His hat trick made him the first player to score four goals in World Cup final matches. His speed and scoring threat as an attacker make him a dominant force on the pitch.

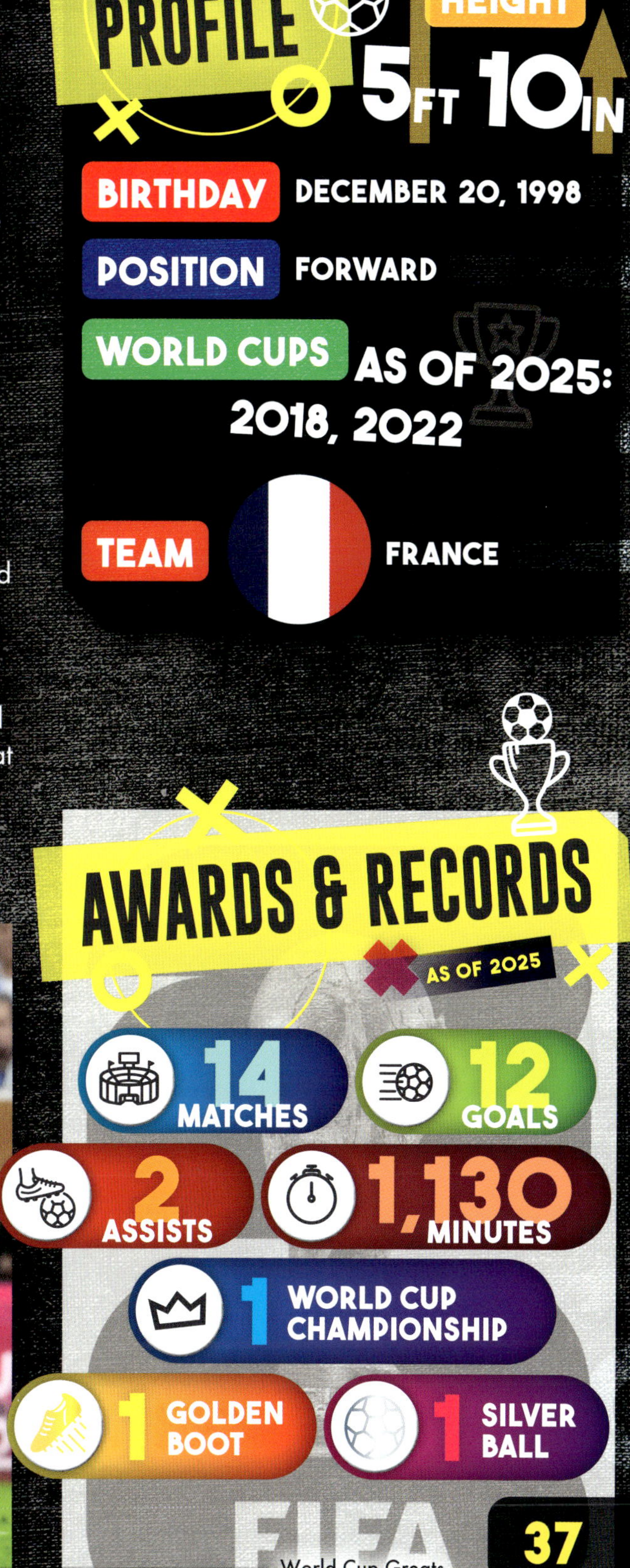

MEMORABLE MOMENTS

BRAZIL'S BEAUTIFUL PLAY

In the 1970 World Cup, Brazil faced Italy in the final. Brazil held onto a 3–1 lead late in the match. At the 86th minute, Brazilian midfielder Tostão stole the ball from Italy. He moved the ball forward to his teammate Brito, who passed it off to Clodoaldo. The ball then got passed in a triangle. Clodoaldo kicked it to Pelé, who passed to Gérson, who sent it back to Clodoaldo.

Clodoaldo dribbled through four defenders. He then passed left to Rivelino, who kicked a long ball straight down the line to Jairzinho. Jairzinho ran at his defender, keeping the ball under perfect control. He cut right and kicked the ball to Pelé in the middle of the field. Pelé eyed Carlos Alberto making a run on the right. He kicked a pass that hit Alberto just as he darted into the **box**. Alberto booted a shot into the air, past Italian goalkeeper Enrico Albertosi, and into the net. The nine-pass play covered nearly the entire pitch. It was the fourth and final goal of the match for Brazil, securing the team's third World Cup title. The spectacular goal has been described as the most beautiful play in World Cup history. The fluid teamwork, creative vision, and outstanding skill of the play illustrates the absolute best of the game.

ALBERTO CELEBRATING GOAL

MARADONA'S GOAL OF THE CENTURY

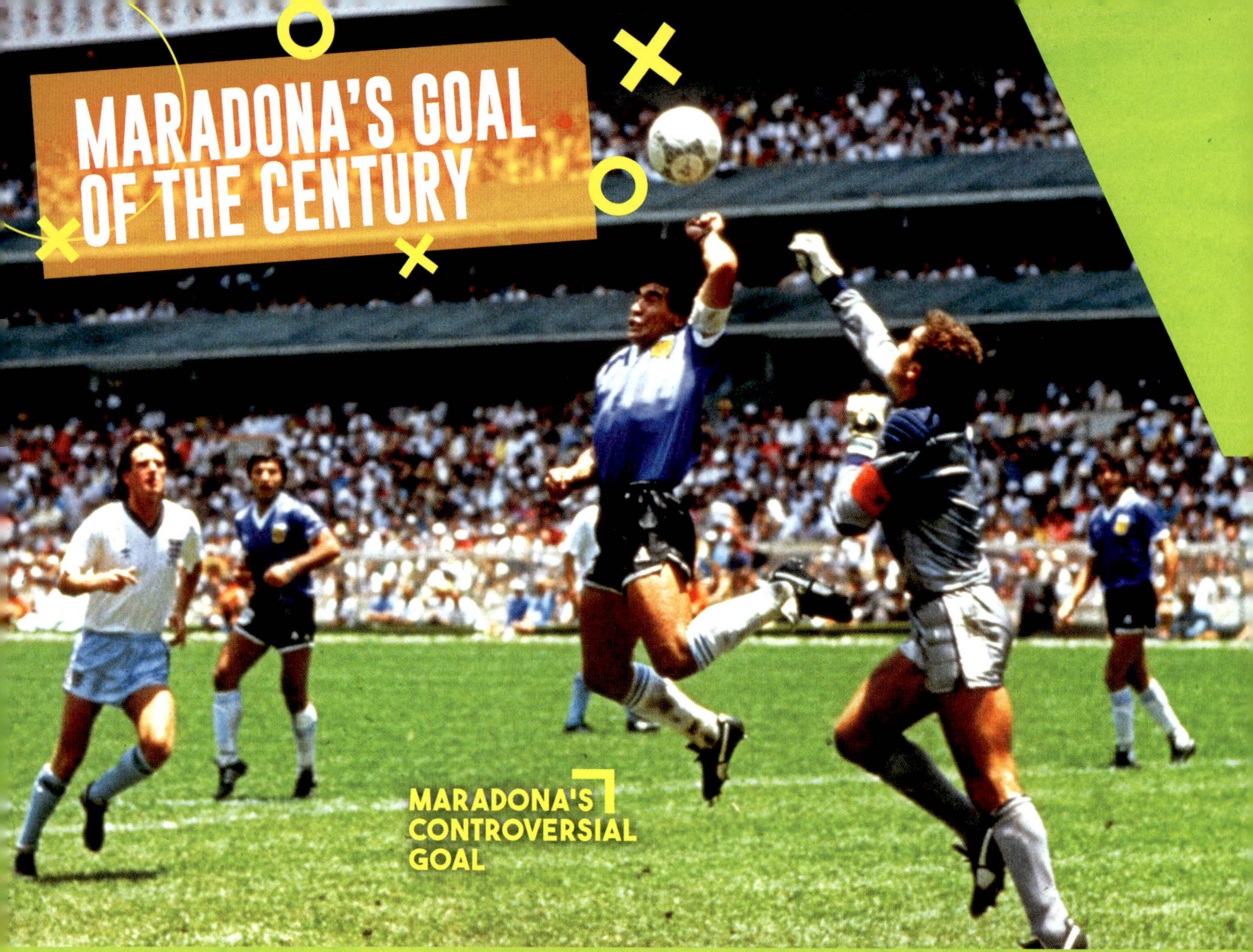

MARADONA'S CONTROVERSIAL GOAL

At the 1986 World Cup quarterfinal, Argentina squared off against England. Early in the second half, Argentina's Diego Maradona scored a controversial goal with his fist. The goal should have been illegal, but the referee thought the ball hit Maradona's head instead of his hand. Down 1–0, England was trying to get back in the match. In the 54th minute, England lost possession to Argentina. The ball was passed to Maradona inside his own half. Maradona dribbled from one end of the pitch to the other, beating every defender along the way. He twisted and turned, moving the ball from his left foot to his right.

After leaping over the leg of England's center back Terry Fenwick, Maradona faced goalkeeper Peter Shilton. Shilton moved off the goal line toward Maradona. England's Terry Butcher slid in to stop Maradona's kick, but he was a fraction of a second too late. The ball sailed into the far corner of the net. Argentina won the match 2–1 and continued all the way to a World Cup title. Maradona's incredible score became known as the "Goal of the Century" and remains one of the greatest goals in World Cup history.

MARADONA'S "GOAL OF THE CENTURY"

BRANDI CHASTAIN'S PENALTY KICK

BRIANA SCURRY SAVING A GOAL

On July 10, 1999, the U.S. faced China in the Women's World Cup final. Over 90,000 fans packed the sold-out Rose Bowl in Pasadena, California. After a scoreless regulation time and overtime, the match went into a penalty shootout.

China scored their first two kicks. But the U.S. matched each score. China's Liu Ying kicked third. Her shot was saved by U.S. goalkeeper Briana Scurry. Next, U.S. midfielder Kristine Lilly kicked past China goalkeeper Gao Hong to give the U.S. the advantage. China scored their next two kicks with the U.S.'s Mia Hamm netting her kick in between. With the score tied 4–4, the U.S. had a chance to win the tournament. Brandi Chastain set the ball on the spot and walked to the edge of the box. She jogged up and smashed it with her left foot. It sailed past Hong's outstretched arms into the upper-right corner of the net. Chastain ripped off her jersey and dropped to her knees in celebration. The rest of the team raced onto the pitch to join her. Chastain's penalty kick became one the greatest moments in Women's World Cup history. The U.S. claimed a 5–4 victory and the 1999 Women's World Cup title.

BRANDI CHASTAIN

PENALTY VICTORIES

Two women's finals and three men's finals have been decided by penalty shootouts.

THE WORLD CUP BY THE NUMBERS
THE FIRST WORLD CUP WAS PLAYED IN 1930.
THE FIRST WOMEN'S WORLD CUP WAS PLAYED IN 1991.
FIFA
AS OF 2025
CAREER GOALS SCORED
MEN
16 GOALS
MIROSLAV KLOSE
WOMEN
17 GOALS
MARTA
CAREER WORLD CUP MATCHES
AS OF 2025
MEN
26 MATCHES
LIONEL MESSI
WOMEN
30 MATCHES
KRISTINE LILLY

FEWEST GOALS ALLOWED IN ONE TOURNAMENT
MEN
0 GOALS ALLOWED IN 2006
PASCAL ZUBERBÜHLER
WOMEN
0 GOALS ALLOWED IN 2007
NADINE ANGERER
MOST GOALS SCORED IN A SINGLE TOURNAMENT
MEN
JUST FONTAINE
13 GOALS IN 1958
WOMEN
MICHELLE AKERS
10 GOALS IN 1991
MOST WORLD CUP TITLES
AS OF 2025
WOMEN
4 TITLES
MEN
5 TITLES
OLDEST TEAMS
ENGLAND 1863
MEN
ITALY 1968
WOMEN

GLOSSARY

berth—a place in a tournament

box—the rectangular area that extends 18 yards (16.5 meters) from each side of the goal and 18 yards (16.5 meters) in front of it; the box is also called the penalty area.

bracket—related to a diagram that represents the series of games played in a tournament

confederations—organizations in charge of all teams from a certain region of the world

draw—a game that ends in a tie

dribbled—moved the ball around the field with small foot touches

group stage—a round of a tournament where teams are placed into groups that they play matches against

hat trick—a soccer achievement in which a player scores three goals in one game

knockout stage—a round of a tournament where the losing team is eliminated from the rest of the tournament

lobbying—attempts to influence a decision

penalty shootout—a way of breaking a tie in a soccer match where teams take penalty kicks until one team scores more than the other

pitch—a soccer field

pots—groupings of teams based on rankings that are used to determine which groups teams are placed in

quadrennial—occurring every four years

regulation time—the regular amount of time a game is played; a full soccer game is 90 minutes long.

saved—stopped a ball from entering the goal

seeds—rankings in a tournament

tactical—related to using skills and acts to accomplish a goal

ticket—a confederation team slot to compete at the World Cup

tournament—a series of games in which several teams try to win the championship

WRITE ABOUT IT!

- **Why** is teamwork so critical in a winning soccer team?
- **What** makes a great soccer player?
- **Which** position do you think is most important to a soccer team?

ALSO CHECK OUT

INDEX

Alberto, Carlos, 18, 38, 39
Argentina, 4, 12, 28, 29, 33, 37, 40, 41
awards, 8–9, 14, 18, 20, 22, 24, 29, 31, 33, 35, 37
Belgium, 12
Brazil, 6, 13, 14, 18, 19, 27, 31, 38
Casillas, Iker, 22, 23
championships, 6, 11, 12, 16, 20, 22
Chastain, Brandi, 42
China, 16, 24, 42
Columbia, 24
confederations, 7, 8
Croatia, 37
Denmark, 12
England, 4, 18, 27, 29, 40, 41
Fédération Internationale de Football Association, 6, 7, 8, 9, 12, 14, 16, 18, 29, 33
FIFA Play-Off Tournament, 8, 9
FIFA World Cup Continental Zones, 7
France, 4, 12, 27, 33, 37
Germany, 14, 20, 21, 22, 24, 29, 33
history, 4, 8, 12, 14, 15, 16, 18, 20, 22, 24, 27, 28, 29, 31, 33, 35, 37, 38, 40, 41, 42, 43
Italy, 16, 18, 27, 38
Jairzinho, 18, 19, 38
Japan, 24, 35
Lloyd, Carli, 24, 25
Maradona, Diego, 28–29, 40, 41
Marta, 30–31
Mbappé, Kylian, 4, 36–37
Messi, Lionel, 4, 5, 32–33
Mexico, 27
Morgan, Alex, 24, 25, 34–35
Müller, Gerd, 20, 21
Netherlands, 12, 20, 22
Norway, 16
Paraguay, 22
Pelé, 18, 19, 26–27, 29, 38
Peru, 18, 37
records, 4, 6, 14, 15, 18, 20, 24, 27, 28, 31, 33, 35, 37
Romania, 29
Spain, 12, 22, 23, 29
Sweden, 12, 27
Switzerland, 12, 22
timeline, 17
Thailand, 35
United States, 6, 16, 24, 25, 29, 35, 42
Uruguay, 12, 18
Wales, 27
World Cup By the Numbers, The, 44–45

The images in this book are reproduced through the courtesy of: ASSOCIATED PRESS/ AP Images, front cover, pp. 1, 2, 3, 4 (Fun fact), 6 (all), 7, 8 (top, Golden Ball, Golden Ball inset), 9 (all), 10 (all), 11, 13 (top), 14 (all), 15 (all), 16 (inset), 17 (1930), 19 (record), 21 (inset), 22 (inset), 25 (record), 28 (main, left), 30 (all), 31, 32 (all), 34 (main, inset, left), 36 (left, right), 37, 38, 39 (all), 42 (all), 43, 44 (Klose, Messi, Lilly), 45 (Angerer, Fontaine), 46 (main), 48 (main); Дмитрий Садовников/ Wikimedia Commons, front cover, p. 1; ZUMA Press, Inc./ Alamy Stock Photo, front cover, pp. 1, 23, 24 (left); PA Images/ Alamy Stock Photo, front cover, pp. 1, 17 (1998), 18, 22, 25 (inset), 28 (right), 29, 35, 40 (inset); fifg, front cover, p. 1; dpa picture alliance/ Alamy Stock Photos, pp. 3, 26; Martin Rickett - PA Images/ Getty Images, p. 4; ADRIAN DENNIS/ Getty Images, p. 5 (top); The Washington Post/ Getty Images, p. 5 (bottom); Wu Zhizhao/ Getty Images, p. 8 (left); Fitria Ramli, pp. 11, 45; Guillermo Laborde/ Wikimedia Commons, p. 12; Gallica Digital Library/ Wikimedia Commons, p. 12 (fun fact); Werner Haberkorn/ Wikimedia Commons, p. 13 (bottom); Bob Thomas/ Getty Images, p. 16; Daniel Motz/ Alamy Stock Photo, pp. 17 (1991), 40 (top), 45 (Akers); FIFA/ Wikimedia Commons, p. 17 (2026); Steve Travelguide, p. 18 (fun fact); Sueddeutsche Zeitung Photo/ Alamy Stock Photo, pp. 19, 26 (left); Action Plus Sports Images/ Alamy Stock Photo, p. 19 (inset); Trinity Mirror/ Mirrorpix/ Alamy Stock Photo, p. 20 (top); Penta Springs Limited/ Alamy Stock Photo, p. 20 (bottom); PA Images Archive/ Getty Images, p. 21; Peter Robinson – EMPICS/ Getty Images, p. 21 (record); Xinhua/ Alamy Stock Photo, p. 24 (right); Jonathan Larsen/ Diadem Images/ Alamy Stock Photo, pp. 25, 44 (Marta); El Gráfico/ Wikimedia Commons, pp. 26 (inset), 27; TT News Agency/ Alamy Stock Photo, p. 26 (right); David Cannon/ Getty Images, p. 28 (inset); Andre Paes/ Alamy Stock Photo, p. 33; dpa picture alliance archive/ Alamy Stock Photo, p. 34 (right); Fabideciria/ Alamy Stock Photo, p. 36 (inset); Aflo Co. Ltd./ Alamy Stock Photo, p. 41 (all); Abaca Press/ Alamy Stock Photo, p. 45 (Zuberbuhler); Rugby pioneers/ Wikimedia Commons, p. 45; Gorodenkoff, pp. 44-45 (background).